TopReaders

Life on Ice

Robert Coupe

Contents

Some animals and humans
live in very cold places.
Ice and snow always cover
the ground. The seas are
never warm. These are
Earth's polar regions .

Icy Waters

Like whales, and also like people,
seals are mammals. They are expert
swimmers and divers. Most seals live
in cold seas in the world's polar regions.
They come ashore to mate and breed.

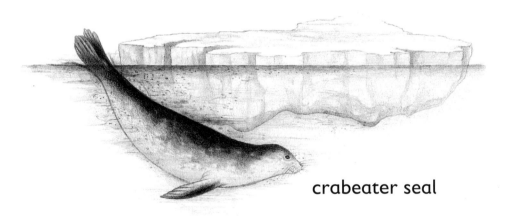

crabeater seal

Baby harp seals are covered in a thick coat of white fur.
This protects the young seal from the extreme cold.
Three weeks after it is born, it sheds this fur coat.

Long Horns

Caribou live in the cold regions
near the North Pole. They eat leaves,
mosses, and grasses. They have antlers
that grow in spring and fall off in winter.
Skin covers the antlers during summer.

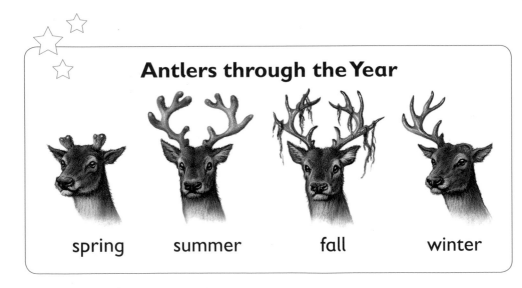

Antlers through the Year

| spring | summer | fall | winter |

A caribou's foot has four toes. When the caribou walks on soft snow, the toes spread out to give a better grip.

antler

caribou

four toes

Bringing up Babies

A polar bear's thick white fur coat
protects it against the winter cold.
Seals are these bears' favorite food.
Males catch them in icy Arctic waters.
Female bears care for the young.

catching
food

mother
and cubs

*A mother bear digs a cave in the snow. Her two babies
stay here with her until they are big enough to go outside.*

Fact File

Polar bear cubs stay with their mothers for two years or more. Then they can look after themselves.

male bears fighting

snow cave

Changing Color

Most foxes have brown or reddish fur.
During the winter, the Arctic fox
has white fur. This makes it hard to see
against the snow. When spring comes,
its fur changes to brown or black.

Summer Fur

An Arctic fox has brown fur in the summer.

In winter, an Arctic fox digs a burrow *deep in the snow.
It goes there to escape from the freezing Arctic winds.*

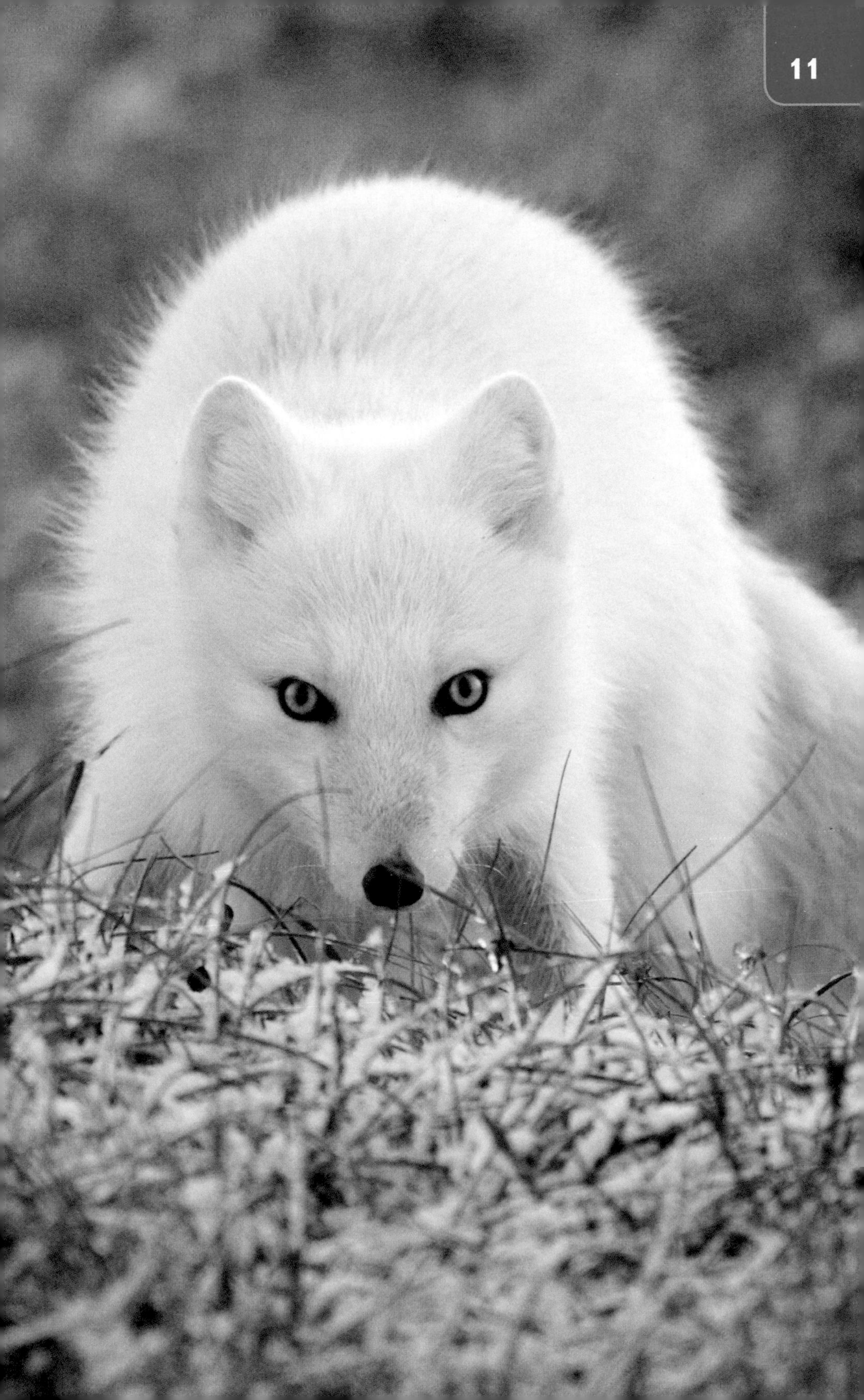

Shaggy Coats

Musk oxen use their long, curved horns
and feet to clear patches in the snow.
That is how they reach the grasses
they eat. They have thick, shaggy coats.
Where they live is cold and often dark.

musk ox

musk oxen

wolf

Wolves are fierce hunters in the cold north of Canada and Alaska. If a hungry wolf comes looking for a meal, adults crowd around to keep a young musk ox safe.

Long-distance Travelers

Many birds make long-distance flights, but the Arctic tern holds the record. Every year, these birds fly right around the world. They fly from near the North Pole to near the South Pole, and then back again.

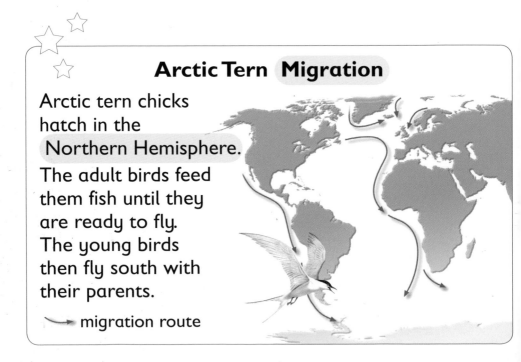

Arctic Tern Migration

Arctic tern chicks hatch in the Northern Hemisphere. The adult birds feed them fish until they are ready to fly. The young birds then fly south with their parents.

→ migration route

Sea Canaries

Belugas are small whales that live and hunt in seas near the North Pole. Large groups of them often swim together. As they move they make chirping sounds. Some people call them "sea canaries."

Fact File

When they are born, belugas are dark gray. As they grow, their color changes. Adults are a creamy white color.

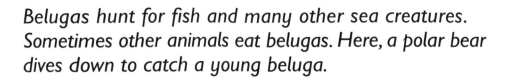

Belugas hunt for fish and many other sea creatures. Sometimes other animals eat belugas. Here, a polar bear dives down to catch a young beluga.

White Hunter

Like all owls, snowy owls are birds of prey.
Lemmings are their favorite food. One owl
can kill up to 10 lemmings in a single day.
If lemmings are scarce, the owls eat mice,
or even young birds.

Fact File

Adult male snowy owls are almost
all white. Adult females have patches
of black on them. Some young owls
are brown with white patches.

*Female snowy owls usually raise lots of chicks.
But when it becomes hard to find enough food,
these owls will not raise any chicks at all.*

Strong Swimmers

Antarctica is the coldest place on Earth.
That is where many penguins live.
These birds cannot fly, but they swim
very strongly. Their thick feathers
help protect them from the cold.

Most birds flap their wings as they fly through the air.
Penguins flap their wings as they swim. They need to swim
fast to escape from seals and some whales that hunt them.

Family Groups

Alaska, in northwest North America, is home to thousands of gray wolves. They live in family groups. They hunt large and small animals. They can run fast and jump high into the air.

Fact File

When gray wolves find a herd of deer, they often pick out the oldest or weakest animal to chase and kill.

Gray wolves can make loud howling sounds. After they kill their prey, they sometimes howl so that other wolves will know where they are.

Working Dogs

People who lived in Arctic regions trained special dogs to pull sleds over ice and snow. These dogs are huskies. Huskies are usually friendly to people. They are strong and have thick fur.

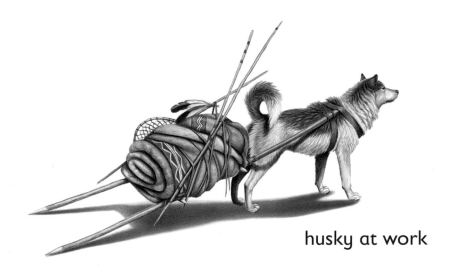

husky at work

Huskies have a strong sense of smell. As well as pulling sleds, they helped people track down animals such as seals.

great auk

No More

Many kinds of animals that once lived no longer exist. Great auks were birds that could not fly. People hunted them for food and to use as bait for fishing. That is why they finally disappeared.

mammoth

About 120,000 years ago, mammoths lived on icy plains. These huge animals died out when the weather got warmer.

Hunters and Fishers

Inuit people live in icy northern regions.
Some Inuits call themselves Eskimos.
There are many Inuits in Alaska
and northern Canada. They used to hunt
with harpoons , but they now use rifles.

snowmobile

In earlier times, Inuit people traveled across the ice
and snow on sleds that were pulled by teams of dogs.
Most Inuits now use snowmobiles, which have motors.

Inuit fishing

Fact File

Inuits made clothes from the skin and fur of seals and deer. They also hunted them for food.

Quiz

Can you unscramble the words and match them with the right pictures?

UYSHK   ORIBUCA

AGERT KAU   TIINU

Glossary

Antarctica: a vast ice-covered land near the South Pole

antlers: large horns that grow on the heads of some animals, such as reindeer

Arctic: in the area near the North Pole

birds of prey: birds that hunt and eat animals with their sharp claws and strong, hooked bill

burrow: a tunnel or hole that an animal digs under the ground to shelter or hide in

caribou: another name for reindeer

great auks: birds that lived long ago. They looked like penguins and could not fly.

harpoons: spears at the end of ropes that people throw or shoot to catch whales and other animals

mammals: animals that drink milk from their mother's body when they are babies

mammoths: large woolly animals that lived long ago and that had a trunk and tusks like an elephant

migration: a very long journey that an animal makes

Northern Hemisphere: the northern half of the world

plains: wide, flat areas of land

polar regions: parts of the world around the North and South poles

Index